FACES ON PLACES

FACES ON PLACES

About Gargoyles and Other Stone Creatures

SUZANNE HALDANE

The Viking Press   New York

To my parents, Nona B. and William R. Haldane,
and my grandmother, Mary Wilson Haldane,
an inspiration to all her grandchildren
and great-grandchildren

Opposite title page: *Larimer Square, Denver, Colorado.*

My sincere thanks to these most dedicated craftsmen:
Malcolm Harlow, René Lavaggi, Roger Morigi,
Constantine Seferlis, Carl Tucker, and Frank Zic.
And thanks to all who helped, especially:
Marc Fetterman, former Assistant Architect,
Washington Cathedral; Bruce Hoheb, Director of
Reproductions, Metropolitan Museum of Art;
Nancy S. Montgomery, Publicity Director, Washington
Cathedral; Karla Held; Dan McCormack; Joan Neary;
Frederick Nicklaus; Jessie Vaught; Jane Wilson
—and most of all, Tom Hyman.   S. H.

First Edition
Copyright © 1980 by Suzanne Haldane
All rights reserved
First published in 1980 by The Viking Press
625 Madison Avenue, New York, N. Y. 10022
Published simultaneously in Canada by
Penguin Books Canada Limited
Printed in U.S.A.
1   2   3   4   5   84   83   82   81   80

Library of Congress Cataloging in Publication Data
Haldane, Suzanne.   Faces on places.
Summary: Describes the work of sculptors,
model makers, stonecutters, and stone carvers in
creating gargoyles and other creatures and surveys
carving on churches and other buildings.
1. Gargoyles—Juvenile literature. 2. Animals,
Mythical, in art—Juvenile literature. 3. Humans in
art—Juvenile literature. 4. Decoration and ornament,
Architectural—Juvenile literature. [1. Gargoyles.
2. Decoration and ornament, Architectural.
3. Sculpture] I. Title.
NA3683.G37H34   729'.5   80–11746
ISBN 0–670–30444–1

FACES ON PLACES

LOOK UP! High above your head all kinds of animals and funny faces are carved on old stone buildings.

These amusing and sometimes scary creatures are in the most unexpected places—on the walls and rooftops of banks, churches, stores, and schools. They are a delight to discover.

Left and right: *Church of the Messiah, Montgomery Street, Rhinebeck, New York.*

7

8

Left: *Washington Cathedral, Washington, D.C.* Above: *Fish gargoyle doing its job as a rain spout, Washington Cathedral.* Above right: *Washington Cathedral.*

All stone carvings are commonly called gargoyles. But gargoyles are really only those animal-like and people-like carvings with wide-open mouths that spit out the rain when it pours. Gargoyles are attached to gutters, where they throw rainwater free of stone walls and help protect buildings from erosion.

The word "gargoyle" is an Old French word meaning throat. Our English word "gargle" comes from the same root.

Above: *Some stone carvings on Notre-Dame Cathedral, Paris, France.* Right: *Notre-Dame Cathedral, Paris, France.*

Gargoyles and carvings that were made in the Middle Ages, more than eight hundred years ago, can still be seen today on cathedrals in Europe. One of the best-known cathedrals is Notre-Dame in Paris, France.

The carvings outside Notre-Dame were made to look as ugly and frightening as possible. If they were ugly enough, it was hoped, they would scare away demons, leaving everyone in the church feeling peaceful and ready for prayer.

Carvings on interior cathedral walls had a different purpose. Since most people in the Middle Ages couldn't read or write, scenes from Bible stories were carved on stone walls to teach religious lessons.

11

Left: *Medieval stone carvers at work. From an illumination of the building of St. Denis Cathedral (seventh century), Paris, France.* Above: *A medieval carver with his tools.* Above right: *The stone carver's tools: mallet, files, chisels, and calipers.*

Paintings, woodcuts, and drawings made during the Middle Ages show how early carvers worked.

They labored many long hours with simple handmade tools: mallets (broad wooden hammers), chisels, files, and calipers for measuring. The same tools are still used to make carvings for buildings today.

13

14

Left: *Formerly 23 West 53rd Street, New York City. This building stood for seventy-five years before it was demolished in 1979.* Above: *Washington Cathedral, Washington, D.C.* Above right: *The Ansonia apartment building, Broadway and 73rd Street, New York City.*

If a stone carving is placed high up on a building, it must be large enough to be seen clearly from the street.

The carver exaggerates the expression on the character's face, just as a circus clown uses makeup to emphasize his own features. Stone carvings often have large, open mouths, deep eyes, bulbous noses, and long, pointed ears.

15

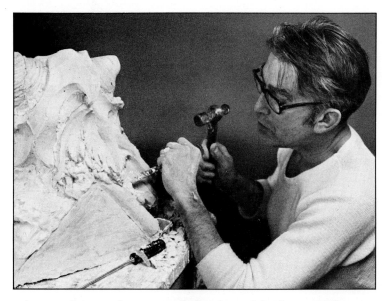

Left: *A sculptor making a small sketch model.* Above: *Carl Tucker, model maker at Washington Cathedral, chips away the mold with a hammer and chisel.*

Four people—*sculptor, model maker, stonecutter,* and *stone carver*—must do a lot of hard work to make a gargoyle.

The *sculptor* begins the piece. His first ideas about a gargoyle take shape in a small clay sketch model.

Then he makes a full-size clay model with the same soft, oil-based clay. He works, making improvements, until the shape is nearly perfect.

Next, the sculptor takes the clay gargoyle to the *model maker.* The model maker will use the clay gargoyle to create a more durable plaster-of-Paris model. As he works, a fine layer of white plaster dust covers the model maker, his tools, and everything else in his shop.

The model maker's effort is like a dress rehearsal for the stone carver. Both use similar tools; both work with great skill and patience. The model maker coats the clay gargoyle with wet plaster and lets it dry. This coating is called the mold. The mold is removed from the no-longer-needed clay form and oiled on the inside. More plaster is poured in. The new plaster will not stick to the oil, so when it has set, the mold is carefully chipped away, leaving the plaster model.

When the model is finished, the model maker takes the hollow plaster model to the *stonecutter.* Selecting a block of limestone that may weigh as much as three hundred pounds, the stonecutter studies the model and roughs out the shape by chipping away the unneeded stone and reducing the block's weight by about half.

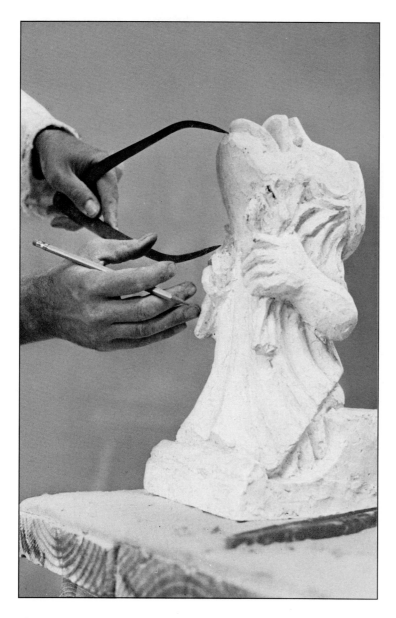

The *stone carver*'s work comes next. His shop, like the model maker's, is covered with dust, but here it is the coarse dust of limestone, the stone most easily carved.

With the limestone block in front of him and the plaster model beside him, the stone carver begins to transfer measurements from the model to the stone. He stretches open a pair of claw-like calipers, places them between two points on the model, and marks off the corresponding points on the stone. After all the measurements have been taken, chiseling begins.

Today stone carvers use a pneumatic chisel, or air hammer, the only tool introduced to stone carving since the Middle Ages.

A rubber hose connects the chisel point with a tank of compressed air. A small motor drives air through the hose, vibrating the chisel point. It is a noisy tool, sounding like the *rat-a-tat-tat* of the jackhammer used in repairing streets, but carvers like it because it makes chiseling faster and less tiring.

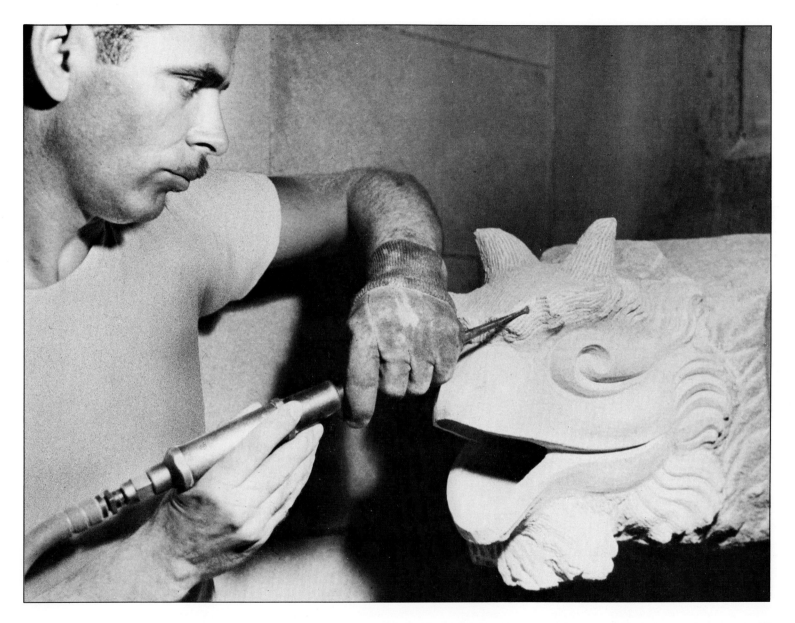

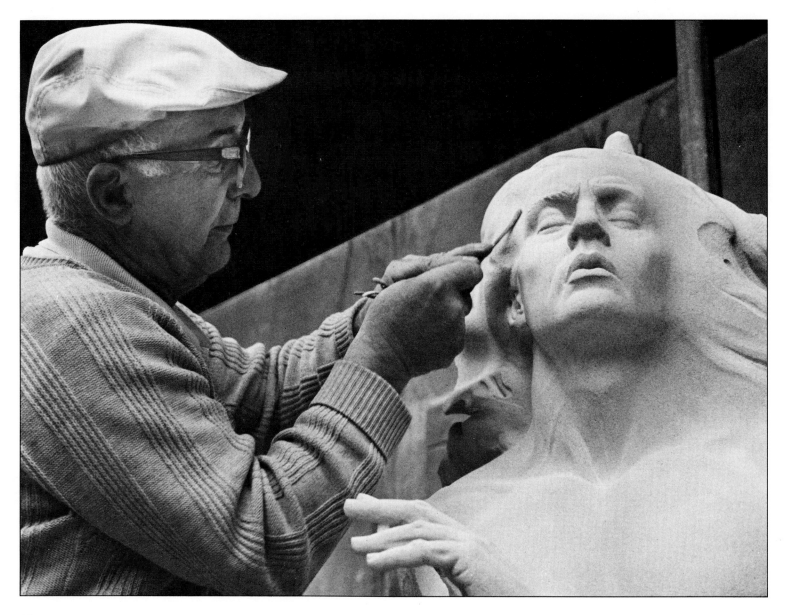

As he works, the stone carver cuts about another fifty pounds off the original limestone block. Then he refines the details with files and small, fine-edged chisels. He must not be in too great a hurry; if he is, he may ruin the stone. In about three weeks the piece is completed.

Today there are only a handful of men who do this kind of work. Most of them are Europeans, many from Italy and Scotland. As young men, they studied art in their homeland and came to the United States in the 1920s when their skill was in great demand. Most have carried on the work of their fathers and grandfathers. Few, if any, women have been stone carvers, but women have been sculptors.

Above: *The west facade of Washington Cathedral, still under construction.* Right: *The south transept entrance.* Far right: *Carvings on the south side of Washington Cathedral.*

It takes a long time to build a cathedral, especially if it is as ornate as some of the cathedrals built in Europe during the Middle Ages. In Washington, D.C., dedicated people are still working to finish a cathedral on which work was begun in 1907. The official name of this grand building is The Cathedral Church of St. Peter and St. Paul, but it is usually called just Washington Cathedral. There will be 106 gargoyles and countless other stone carvings on this building when it is finished.

24

Left: *Stone carving of a dentist on the ground outside the stone carvers' workshop.* Right: *Some personal carvings on Washington Cathedral.*

The money to build Washington Cathedral comes from private donations. Anyone donating $1800 can have a gargoyle carved and dedicated to a family, a friend, or even a pet. Many personal stories and mementos have been carved there in stone.

Money for one gargoyle was given by a dentist, which inspired a sculptor to make an amusing carving of a dentist polishing a mammoth walrus tusk.

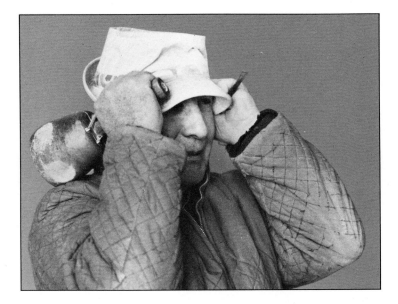

Above left: *Morigi posing as the gargoyle of himself.* Above: *The Morigi gargoyle.* Right: *293 Madison Avenue, New York City.*

One of the gargoyles on Washington Cathedral is modeled after Roger Morigi, the master carver. His fellow workers joke about his quick temper and demand for perfection. One of them designed and carved a gargoyle of Morigi "blowing his top." The gargoyle figure of Morigi holds his carving tools as he clutches the brim of his hat. From the top of his hat spouts an eruption like an exploding atomic bomb.

There are many carvings that tell stories.
Carvers have fun playing jokes on their friends
by carving them in stone. Sometimes their sense
of humor is obvious.

28

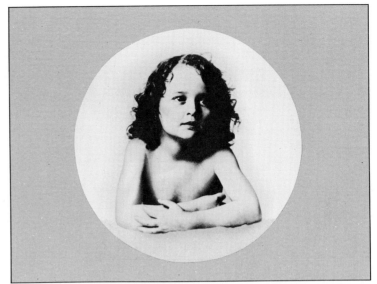

Far left: *The Eastern Stairway of the New York State Capitol, Albany, New York.* Left: *Carving of Lucretia Perry.* Above: *Lucretia Perry in the late 1800s.*

One carving on the state capitol of New York, in Albany, shows a black man holding his head high above the links of a broken chain. Made after the Civil War, this carving symbolizes the end of slavery in the United States.

A more personal carving portrays a young girl named Lucretia, the granddaughter of Isaac Perry, the architect who cared most about stone carvings for the capitol. Now her own grandchildren can see her gazing at them.

Left: *36 West 73rd Street, New York City.* Above: *100 East 24th Street, New York City.* Above right: *20 East 65th Street, New York City.* Far right: *Originally on a building in Chicago, this carving is now in the Brooklyn Museum Sculpture Garden, Brooklyn, New York.*

There is a lot of variety in stone carvings. Some of the most exciting are of animals, but many carvings look like a combination of animals and people. And sometimes leaves and plants form the whole shape of a head.

Cathedral of St. John the Divine, New York City.

Riverside Church, New York City.

The cat is considered independent, quiet, passive—and sometimes lazy. Making himself into a complete circle by biting his own tail, this cat symbolizes eternal laziness.

With the head and body of a lion and the wings of an eagle, the imaginary griffin represents courage and heroism.

Apartment building at 730 Park Avenue, New York City.

*Alwyn Court apartment building,
180 West 58th Street, New York City.*

Strong and forceful, the ram adds strength to sturdy stone buildings.

According to myths, the salamander can resist fire, and so he symbolizes those who can resist temptation. The salamander was the personal emblem of Francis I of France and can be seen on many buildings in France.

The fencing around this carving keeps pigeons from roosting.

33

34

Left: *The goddess Minerva with lions on her helmet. Myths tell us that she protects the homeland. State Capitol of West Virginia, Charleston, West Virginia.* Above left: *Lockhart Hall, Princeton University, Princeton, New Jersey.* Above right: *232 Madison Avenue, New York City.* Bottom right: *New York State Capitol, Albany, New York.*

The lion is the animal most frequently carved on buildings. As the "king of the beasts," the lion's presence suggests majesty, strength, courage, and protection. In folktales lions—always on guard—sleep with their eyes wide open.

Left: *233 East 37th Street, New York City.* Above: *372 Park Avenue South, New York City.*

Since new stone carvings are rarely made today, we must do all we can to protect and save the ones we have. But the task is not easy.

Some carvings look as if they had been dipped into a bath of black dye. They have been badly discolored by the particles that float around in polluted air and cling stubbornly to stonework.

Chemicals found in city air slowly eat away stone. In winter the sulfur oxides released by fuels burned for heating destroy the carvings.

The Brooklyn Museum in Brooklyn, New York, displays some carvings that were saved from demolition all over the country. In the Frieda Schiff Warburg Memorial Sculpture Garden there are more than a hundred carvings. Some of them rest on the ground, nearly smothered in ivy.

Below and right: *Frieda Schiff Warburg Memorial Sculpture Garden, Brooklyn, New York.*

Left: *Above stylized cactus, prospectors pan for gold. Cochise County Courthouse, Bisbee, Arizona.* Right: *224 West 57th Street, New York City.*

This book is a sampling of some of the stone carvings that have been lovingly designed and placed on buildings. There are many more to see. Once you find one, you'll discover another, then another, then another, and each one you find will be a treasure—a piece of the past, something worth saving, and a storyteller.

PHOTO CREDITS

page 2: Joan Neary

page 8: Stewart Brothers, Inc., from *Sculpture and Carving at Washington Cathedral* by Richard T. Feller, edited by Nancy S. Montgomery; © 1976 by the Protestant Episcopal Cathedral Foundation.

page 9: *Left:* Courtesy Washington Cathedral. *Right:* Stewart Brothers, Inc., from *Sculpture and Carving at Washington Cathedral* by Richard T. Feller, edited by Nancy S. Montgomery; © 1976 by the Protestant Episcopal Cathedral Foundation.

page 10: Culver Pictures, Inc.

page 11: Courtesy New York Public Library

page 12: Bibliothèque Nationale, Paris

page 13: *Left:* Courtesy New York Public Library

page 15: *Left:* Stewart Brothers, Inc., from *Sculpture and Carving at Washington Cathedral* by Richard T. Feller, edited by Nancy S. Montgomery; © 1976 by the Protestant Episcopal Cathedral Foundation.

page 19: Stewart Brothers, Inc.

page 25: H. Byron Chambers from *Sculpture and Carving at Washington Cathedral* by Richard T. Feller, edited by Nancy S. Montgomery; © 1976 by the Protestant Episcopal Cathedral Foundation.

page 26: *Right:* Stewart Brothers, Inc., from *Sculpture and Carving at Washington Cathedral* by Richard T. Feller, edited by Nancy S. Montgomery; © 1976 by the Protestant Episcopal Cathedral Foundation.

page 29: *Left:* Arthur John Daley from *Capitol Story* by Cecil R. Roseberry, with photographs by Arthur John Daley; © 1964 by the State of New York.

page 31: *Left:* The author from *The New York Kid's Book: 170 Children's Writers and Artists Celebrate New York City;* © 1979 by The New York Kid's Catalog, a New York Partnership.

page 37: *Left:* The author from *Parabola* magazine, Vol. IV, No. 4; © 1979 by the Society for the Study of Myth and Tradition. Photograph © 1979, Suzanne Haldane.

page 38: Joan Neary

All other photographs by the author. Photographs have not been previously published, except as noted.

81 Irving Place, New York City.